English
Rapid Tests 6

Siân Goodspeed

Schofield & Sims

Introduction

This book gives you practice in answering English questions quickly.

The questions are like the questions on the 11+ and other school selection tests. You must find the correct answers.

School selection tests are usually timed, so you need to get used to working quickly. Each test has a target time for you to work towards. You should time how long you spend on each test, or you can ask an adult to time you.

What you need

- A pencil
- An eraser
- A clock, watch or stopwatch
- An adult to mark the test for you

What to do

- Turn to **Section 1 Test 1** on page 4. Look at the grey box at the top of the page labelled **Target time**. This tells you how long the test should take.
- When you are ready to start, write down the time or start the stopwatch. Or the adult helping you will tell you to begin.
- Read each question carefully and then write the answer on the answer line. Always write in full sentences, except where the question tells you otherwise. Sometimes you need to tick or underline the correct answer instead.
- Try to answer every question. If you do get stuck on a question, leave it and go on to the next one. Work quickly and try your best.
- Each test is two pages long. When you reach the end, stop. Write down the time or stop the stopwatch. Or tell the adult that you have finished.
- Work out how long you took to do the test. Fill in the **Time taken** box at the end of the test.
- The adult will mark your test and fill in the **Score** and **Target met?** boxes.
- Turn to the **Progress chart** on page 40. Write your score in the box and colour in the graph to show how many questions you got right.
- Did you get some questions wrong? You should always have another go at them before you look at the answers. Then ask the adult to check your work and help you if you are still not sure.
- When you have finished working through this book, and are able to answer the questions both rapidly and correctly, you will be well prepared for school selection tests.

Published by **Schofield & Sims Ltd**,
7 Mariner Court, Wakefield, West Yorkshire WF4 3FL, UK
Telephone 01484 607080
www.schofieldandsims.co.uk

This edition copyright © Schofield & Sims Ltd, 2018
First published in 2018
Second impression 2020

Author: **Siân Goodspeed**. Siân Goodspeed has asserted her moral rights under the Copyright, Designs and Patents Act, 1988, to be identified as the author of this work.

How to make a cockroach robot (page 4) is based on a project by BrownDogGadgets.com. Original project and kit created by BrownDogGadgets.com. **Coram Boy** (pages 10 and 11) is an extract from Coram Boy by Jamila Gavin published by Egmont Books. Used with permission from David Higham Associates. **The Carnivorous Carnival** (pages 16 and 17) is an extract from A Series of Unfortunate Events: The Carnivorous Carnival by Lemony Snicket. Text copyright © 2002 Lemony Snicket. Published by Egmont UK Limited and used with permission. **Scientists zapped people's brains...** (page 22) is an extract from The Independent. Josh Gabbatiss © The Independent, Weds 22 November, 2017. **The Listeners** (page 28) is an extract from The Listeners by Walter de la Mare. Used with permission from The Literary Trustees of Walter de la Mare and The Society of Authors as their representative. **Monster** (page 34) is an extract from Monster by Michael Grant. Text copyright © 2017 Michael Grant. Published by Egmont UK Ltd and used with permission.

Every effort has been made to trace all copyright holders and obtain their permission to reproduce copyright material prior to publication. If notified, the publisher will rectify any errors or omissions at the earliest opportunity.

British Library Cataloguing in Publication Data. A catalogue record for this book is available from the British Library.

All rights reserved. No part of this publication may be reproduced, stored in a retrieval system, or transmitted in any form or by any means, electronic, mechanical, photocopying, recording or otherwise, without either the prior permission of the publisher or a licence permitting restricted copying in the United Kingdom issued by the Copyright Licensing Agency Ltd.

Design by **Ledgard Jepson Ltd**
Front cover design by **Ledgard Jepson Ltd**
Printed in the UK by **Page Bros (Norwich) Ltd**

ISBN 978 07217 1434 9

Contents

Section 1	**Test 1**	Comprehension	4
	Test 2	Grammar and punctuation	6
	Test 3	Spelling and vocabulary	8
	Test 4	Comprehension	10
	Test 5	Grammar and punctuation	12
	Test 6	Spelling and vocabulary	14
Section 2	**Test 1**	Comprehension	16
	Test 2	Grammar and punctuation	18
	Test 3	Spelling and vocabulary	20
	Test 4	Comprehension	22
	Test 5	Grammar and punctuation	24
	Test 6	Spelling and vocabulary	26
Section 3	**Test 1**	Comprehension	28
	Test 2	Grammar and punctuation	30
	Test 3	Spelling and vocabulary	32
	Test 4	Comprehension	34
	Test 5	Grammar and punctuation	36
	Test 6	Spelling and vocabulary	38
Progress chart			40

A **pull-out answers section** (pages A1 to A12) appears in the centre of this book, between pages 20 and 21. It also gives simple guidance on how best to use this book. Remove this section before the child begins working through the tests.

Section 1 Test 1

Comprehension

Target time: **8 minutes**

Read the text and answer the questions below.

How to make a cockroach robot (based on a project by BrownDogGadgets.com)

You have probably seen robots in movies about the future, but how much more exciting would it be to make one? Follow the instructions below to build your own solar-powered robot insect.

What you will need:
- A small solar panel – you can buy this cheaply online
- A vibrating motor – try to get one that will only need a small amount of power, so that you can play with your robot even on cloudy days
- Two paper clips
- A pair of googly eyes
- Wire
- A soldering iron and solder
- A hot glue gun
- Wire cutters or strong scissors.

Method:
1. Solder a piece of wire to each side of the motor, taking care not to melt the motor with the heat from the solder gun.
2. Align the two wires with the solar panel and solder together.
3. To make the cockroach's legs, uncoil the paper clips and then bend them into 'V' shapes.
4. Glue the legs on to the motor but do not let them touch the wires! It will damage the motor if electricity runs through it.
5. You can now customise your cockroach robot by adding the googly eyes. You could also attach a pair of antennae made from wire to make him or her even more adorable!

Write **A**, **B**, **C** or **D** on the answer line.

1. Why is the robot described as 'solar-powered'?
   A It works by using energy from the sun.
   B It is happier when the weather is good.
   C It uses a battery for power.
   D It moves speedily.

   _____ /1

2. Which piece of equipment is optional?
   A soldering iron
   B strong scissors
   C motor
   D solar panel

   _____ /1

3. Which word is a synonym for 'customise'?
   A purchase
   B personalise
   C enlarge
   D inspire

   _____ /1

4. How much should you expect to pay for the solar panel?
   A not very much
   B a large amount of money
   C nothing at all
   D more than you can afford

   _____ /1

Comprehension — Section 1 Test 1 continued

5. Why do you think it is a sensible idea to use a motor that does not need high levels of power?

   _____

   _____ /2

6. What **two** mistakes do the instructions warn you against making?

   _____

   _____ /2

7. Do you need to follow the fifth instruction in order to make the robot? Explain your answer.

   _____

   _____ /2

8. Write **two** imperative verbs from the text. Explain why these verbs are used for instructions.

   _____

   _____ /2

9. Give **two** ways in which the layout of the text is designed to make the instructions easy to follow for the reader, and explain how each achieves this goal.

   _____

   _____ /2

10. The following text is a set of instructions for playing a trick on your friends using your cockroach robot. Some of the words have been removed. Choose the word that best fits and write it on the line. Not all the words are needed and you may use each word only once.

    | upturned | distinct | confront | stomping | frenzied | gigantic |
    | collision | scuttling | springs | position | enjoyment | mayhem |

    a) _____ your robot beneath an b) _____ mug.

    When your friends arrive, burst into a c) _____ explanation of how

    you trapped a d) _____ beetle that was e) _____

    around the kitchen. Ask which one of them is brave enough to f) _____

    the beast and ask them to lift up the mug. Watch the g) _____ unfold

    as the sunlight hits the solar panel of your robot and it h) _____ into life! /8

Score: _____ Time taken: _____ Target met? _____

Section 1 Test 2

Grammar and punctuation

Target time: **8 minutes**

1. Change the missing verb to the tense given in brackets to complete each sentence. Write the missing verb form on the line.

   Example: Li (help) _was helping_ her dad with the dinner. (PAST PROGRESSIVE)

   a) I (travel) _____ to work on the bus. (PRESENT PROGRESSIVE)

   b) Last week, we (go) _____ to the art gallery. (SIMPLE PAST)

   c) Gina (spend) _____ all her savings. (PRESENT PERFECT)

   d) Toby (eat) _____ his whole packed lunch – and it wasn't even 11.00 a.m! (PAST PERFECT)

   /4

2. Each sentence below is missing <u>two</u> items of punctuation. Correct the sentences.

   a) Theo works in the library his brother Daniel, works in the supermarket.

   b) Michaela's car is fast Almas car is even faster!

   c) The large sign had the words KEEP OUT! painted on it in red.

   d) The buffet was delicious and included the following three types of salad two platters of sandwiches and an assortment of desserts.

   /4

3. Turn each word into an abstract noun by changing its suffix. Write the new word on the line.

   Example: happy ⟶ _happiness_

   a) believed ⟶ _____

   b) wondering ⟶ _____

   c) anxious ⟶ _____

   d) excited ⟶ _____

   e) jealous ⟶ _____

   f) grieves ⟶ _____

   /6

Grammar and punctuation

Section **1** Test **2**
continued

4. In each of the sentences below, two of the words have swapped places. Work out which words need to be swapped for the sentence to make sense. Underline the two words.

  Example: Her <u>was</u> food <u>favourite</u> pasta.

  a) After the debris, there were countless pieces of shipwreck in the ocean.

  b) Buddy the dog was at skilful fetching the stick when Sally threw it for him.

  c) During the next session, the politicians decided to law a new institute.

  d) Saturday tennis was her favourite way to pass a playing afternoon.

/4

5. Some of the following sentences contain a punctuation error. If you spot an error, circle the letter above it and then write out that part of the sentence correctly on the line. If there is no error, write **no error** on the line.

a)

A	B	C	D	E
I want to go	on holiday	somewhere	hot sunny,	and exotic.

_____

b)

A	B	C	D	E
"Please may	I have a slice	of roulade?"	enquired	Owen.

_____

c)

A	B	C	D	E
Hannah was	older than	her sister, Mel	but she was	much shorter.

_____

d)

A	B	C	D	E
"I aspire to be	an Astronaut	when I grow	up," declared	Lucie.

_____

/4

Score:	Time taken:	Target met?

English Rapid Tests 6

7

Section 1 Test 3

Spelling and vocabulary

Target time: **8 minutes**

1. Underline the word in each set of brackets that is an antonym of the word in bold.

   Example: peak (wide   <u>trough</u>   tall)

   a) **profound**   (important   superficial   discovery)

   b) **bleak**   (joyful   consolation   stormy)

   c) **tumult**   (tranquillity   confusing   rough)

   d) **soporific**   (dull   soggy   invigorating)

   /4

2. Underline the word in each set of brackets that is a synonym of the word in bold.

   Example: dull (bright   chilly   <u>dismal</u>)

   a) **domicile**   (assert   dwelling   manifest)

   b) **soppy**   (sentimental   ugly   discontent)

   c) **epitome**   (book   epitaph   essence)

   d) **judicious**   (judgemental   prudent   difficult)

   /4

3. Write these words as an abbreviation on the line.

   Example: Saint   _St._

   a) et cetera   _____

   b) Road   _____

   c) ounce   _____

   d) Captain   _____

   /4

Spelling and vocabulary

Section **1** Test **3**
continued

4. Some of the following sentences contain a spelling error. If you spot an error, circle the letter above it and then write the correct spelling on the line. If there is no error, write **no error** on the line.

a)

A	B	C	D	E
Selina hoped	her exam	results would	be more than	adaquate.

_____

b)

A	B	C	D	E
Jo's work	environment	was rife with	predjudice and	discrimination.

_____

c)

A	B	C	D	E
The desert is	an extremely	barren and	dessolate	landscape.

_____

d)

A	B	C	D	E
Anil's inaugural	pilgrimage to	Nepal was	a voyage of	self-discovery.

_____

/4

5. Write an appropriate collective noun on the line to complete each phrase.

Example: a _flock_ of sheep

a) a _____ of ships

b) a _____ of flies

c) a _____ of dancers

d) a _____ of mountains

e) a _____ of stairs

f) a _____ of kittens

/6

Score: Time taken: Target met?

English Rapid Tests 6   9

Section 1 Test 4

Comprehension

Target time: **8 minutes**

Read the text and answer the questions below.

Extract from **Coram Boy, by Jamila Gavin**

"Oi! Meshak! Wake up, you lazy dolt!" The sound of the rough voice set the dogs barking. "Can't you see one of the panniers is slipping on that mule there! Not that one, you nincompoop," as the boy leapt guiltily from the wagon and darted in an agitated way among the overloaded animals, "that one – there – fifth one back! Yes. Fool of a boy. Why was I so
5 cursed with a son like you? I don't have to have eyes in the back of my head to know that one of the mules had his load slipping. What goes on inside that addled brain of yours?"

A man and his boy were coming out of the forest with a wagon and train of six mules. They were heading for the ferry at Framilodes Passage, which would take them across the River Severn and on to the city of Gloucester.

10 "Why I don't ditch you is more than I can say. Thank your lucky stars that blood is thicker than water. Tighten him up properly. Don't want no hold ups now. We can just catch the ferry before nightfall if we hurry!"

Otis Gardiner, pots man, Jack-of-all-trades and smooth-tongued entrepreneur, ranted non-stop. It was a side of Otis that not everyone saw; he could be so attractive, so charming, so sweetly
15 spoken. A young man still, he had wide, appealing, brown eyes and shoulder-length red-brown hair drawn back to show off his broad, handsome brow. He could barter the hind leg off a donkey – especially if the donkey was a lady. By flirting with the wives, bantering with the gentlemen, demonstrating magic tricks to little children, he could persuade a customer to part with twice as much money as they should, all the while making them think they had themselves
20 a bargain.

Write **A**, **B**, **C** or **D** on the answer line.

1. What relation is Meshak to Otis Gardiner?
   A Meshak is his father.
   B Meshak is his brother.
   C Meshak is his son.
   D Meshak is his cousin.

   _____ /1

2. What does Otis Gardiner do for a living?
   A He is a ferryman.
   B He is a hairdresser.
   C He is a magician.
   D He is a salesman.

   _____ /1

3. What is Meshak and Otis's final destination?
   A the ferry
   B Framilodes Passage
   C the River Severn
   D the city of Gloucester

   _____ /1

4. Which word is a synonym for 'agitated'?
   A leisurely
   B anxious
   C ferocious
   D agile

   _____ /1

Comprehension

Section **1** Test **4**
continued

5. Why did Meshak leap 'guiltily' from the wagon?

_____

_____ /2

6. Find <u>two</u> examples of informal language, such as vocabulary or sentence structure, in lines 1–4.

_____ and _____ /2

7. In line 10, what does Otis mean by, "Thank your lucky stars that blood is thicker than water."?

_____

_____ /2

8. Reread the final paragraph. Why is Otis described as 'smooth-tongued'?

_____

_____ /2

9. How does Otis 'persuade a customer to part with twice as much money as they should'?

_____

_____ /2

10. The following passage is also from *Coram Boy*, but it has had some words removed. Choose the word that best fits and write it on the line. Not all the words are needed and you may use each word only once.

| dangled | vulnerable | stared | fumbled | awkward | slunk |
| capable | incomprehension | cuffed | swaggered | confident | jeered |

His arms and legs **a)** _____ from his body, uncoordinated and clumsy; he dropped things, tripped over things, **b)** _____ and stumbled. All this meant that people – especially his father – shouted at him, **c)** _____ him, **d)** _____ and sneered at him, so his whole look was that of a cowering dog. If he had had a tail, it would have always been between his legs, as he **e)** _____ by waiting for the next kick. He had a **f)** _____, infantile look, with his pale-freckled face beneath a stack of wild red hair, and his large, watery, blue eyes, which often **g)** _____ round at the world with **h)** _____. /8

Score: ____ Time taken: ____ Target met? ____

English Rapid Tests 6   11

Section 1 Test 5

Grammar and punctuation

Target time: 8 minutes

1. The following passage is missing some punctuation. Add in the missing punctuation.

   Hurry up, Joshi! called his mother. You don't want to be late for school not again! Joshi rolled out of bed bleary-eyed and with ruffled hair and staggered to the bathroom to wash his face. He caught a glimpse of himself in the mirror and was shocked at how tired he looked he had bags under his eyes the size of potato sacks Well, that's what comes of staying up half the night on the Xbox he thought to himself.

   /6

2. Decide which of the words in bold is the correct word to complete the sentence in Standard English. Underline the word.

   a) Would you pass me **them / those** books, please?

   b) She finished her dinner and dashed **quick / quickly** out of the door.

   c) My gran could **have / of** been a ballerina.

   d) The police officer said that she didn't want **no / any** trouble.

   /4

3. Write an adverb based on each phrase on the line.

   Example: with happiness ⟶ *happily*

   a) with envy ⟶ _____
   b) in hunger ⟶ _____
   c) with joy ⟶ _____
   d) by mistake ⟶ _____

   /4

12

Schofield & Sims

Grammar and punctuation

Section **1** Test **5**
continued

4. The words in the sentences below have been jumbled up and an extra word has been added in that is not needed. Unjumble the sentences in your head so they make sense, and write the extra word on the line.

   Example: which yours when hat is?   _when_

   a) light the combust first that quickly kindling fire to get burning.   _____

   b) they Susie leader her for shrewd greatly admired judgement.   _____

   c) his friend best went to a shops to the presents buy for he.   _____

   d) "what of American knows accent kind does he?" he have asked.   _____

   /4

5. Some of the following sentences contain a punctuation error. If you spot an error, circle the letter above it and then write out that part of the sentence correctly on the line. If there is no error, write **no error** on the line.

   a)

A	B	C	D	E
Mia was	shocked at	the rudeness	of her sisters	friend.

   _____

   b)

A	B	C	D	E
My younger	brother loves	art classes	I prefer	sport.

   _____

   c)

A	B	C	D	E
That's enough!	the angry	father shouted	at his noisy	son.

   _____

   d)

A	B	C	D	E
"Is that	dress too	expensive?"	Priya asked	her mum.

   _____

   /4

Score: _____   Time taken: _____   Target met? _____

English Rapid Tests 6

Section 1 Test 6

Spelling and vocabulary

Target time: 8 minutes

1. One word from the first set of brackets goes together with one word from the second set of brackets to make a new word. Underline the two words and write the new word on the line.

   Example: (<u>in</u> out about)   (<u>to</u> game of)   <u>into</u>

   a) (cut pie toy)   (yak let lots)   _____

   b) (gold con globe)   (tour piece spin)   _____

   c) (special adapt try)   (effect all able)   _____

   d) (in guard pry)   (din slave mate)   _____

   e) (down gum turn)   (ant tube cast)   _____

   f) (net big pop)   (chips pies fish)   _____

   /6

2. Write out the words in each row on the line so that they are in alphabetical order.

   Example: play place ploy plea plant   <u>place plant play plea ploy</u>

   a) glue glee glide glance glower
   _____

   b) bream brawl breeze brawn break
   _____

   c) through threat thrill thread thrice
   _____

   d) martyr marina marvel marvellous mariner
   _____

   /4

14   Schofield & Sims

Spelling and vocabulary

Section **1** Test **6**
continued

3. The following words are spelt incorrectly. Write the correct spelling on the line.

a) vaxeen _____

b) intervine _____

c) routene _____

d) cantean _____

/4

4. Read the definitions and complete the words that go with them.

a) in a very unhappy state   ___ ___ ___**tched**

b) one of the first to explore an area   ___ ___ ___**neer**

c) to voluntarily leave a job   **res**___ ___ ___

d) to give something in order to help achieve something   **contr**___ ___ ___**te**

/4

5. Decide which of the words in bold is the correct homophone for each sentence. Underline the word.

Example: My house is just over **there** / **they're**.

a) Over the fireplace, in a large **guilt** / **gilt** frame, hung a portrait of his great-grandfather.

b) The farmer collected several **bales** / **bails** of hay to feed his horses.

c) The **flew** / **flue** is the part of the chimney that lets smoke out of a building.

d) Sarah **rued** / **rude** the day she had 'borrowed' her sister's top, as now all of hers had gone missing.

/4

Score:	Time taken:	Target met?

Section 2 Test 1

Comprehension

Target time: **8 minutes**

Read the text and answer the questions below.

Extract from **The Carnivorous Carnival, by Lemony Snicket**

When my workday is over, and I have closed my notebook, hidden my pen, and sawed holes in my rented canoe so that it cannot be found, I often like to spend the evening in conversation with my few surviving friends. Sometimes we discuss literature. Sometimes we discuss the people who are trying to destroy us, and if there is any hope of escaping
5   from them. And sometimes we discuss frightening and troublesome animals that might be nearby, and this topic always leads to much disagreement over which part of a frightening and troublesome beast is the most frightening and troublesome. Some say the teeth of the beast, because teeth are used for eating children, and often their parents, and gnawing their bones. Some say the claws of the beast, because claws are
10 used for ripping things to shreds. And some say the hair of the beast, because hair can make allergic people sneeze.

But I always insist that the most frightening part of any beast is its belly, for the simple reason that if you are seeing the belly of the beast it means you have already seen the teeth of the beast and the claws of the beast and even the hair of the beast, and now
15 you are trapped and there is probably no hope for you. For this reason, the phrase 'in the belly of the beast' has become an expression which means 'inside some terrible place with little chance of escaping safely,' and it is not an expression one should look forward to using.

Write **A**, **B**, **C** or **D** on the answer line.

1. Which of the following is <u>not</u> something the author says he does at the end of a workday?
   A writes in his notebook
   B hides his pen
   C holds conversations with his friends
   D saws holes in his canoe

   _____ /1

2. Which adjective describes the author's friends?
   A argumentative
   B alive
   C troublesome
   D allergic

   _____ /1

3. Which of these is <u>not</u> referred to as frightening?
   A the teeth of the beast
   B the belly of the beast
   C the claws of the beast
   D the eyes of the beast

   _____ /1

4. What type of figurative language is the phrase 'in the belly of the beast'?
   A metaphor
   B simile
   C idiom
   D personification

   _____ /1

Comprehension
Section 2 Test 1 continued

5. Why do you think sawing holes in the canoe would mean it couldn't be found?
   _____
   _____ /2

6. List <u>two</u> topics of conversation the author says he has with his friends.
   _____
   _____ /2

7. Why do some of the author's friends fear the teeth of the beast?
   _____
   _____ /2

8. Why does the author think the belly is the most frightening part of the beast?
   _____
   _____ /2

9. Which <u>two</u> words best describe the atmosphere created by the author in this passage? Tick the boxes.

   ominous ☐   whimsical ☐   humorous ☐   mystical ☐   joyful ☐   /2

10. The following passage is an extract from later in the story, but it has had some words removed. Underline the correct word in bold to complete the passage.

    The Baudelaire a) **delinquent / feuds / orphans** were in the belly of the beast – that is, in the dark and b) **capacious / cramped / cavernous** trunk of a long, black automobile. Unless you are a small, c) **prolific / pensive / portable** object, you probably prefer to sit in a seat when you are traveling by automobile, so you can lean back against the d) **upholstery / upheaval / upholding**, look out the window at the e) **site / scenery / scenic** going by, and feel safe and secure with a seat belt f) **fastened / fastener / fastens** low and tight across your lap. But the Baudelaires could not lean back, and their bodies were aching from squishing up against one another for several hours. They had no window to look out of, only a few bullet holes in the trunk made from some violent g) **encouragement / encounter / enrage** I have not found the courage to h) **receive / resurrect / research**. /8

| Score: | Time taken: | Target met? |

English Rapid Tests 6   17

Section 2 Test 2

Grammar and punctuation

Target time: 8 minutes

1. Sort each word in the word bank into the correct word class by writing it in the table below. You may use each word only once.

   Word bank

gaggle	considerate	band	confidence
despair	trust	solemnly	murder
ambitious	host	immense	wildly
seldom	promptly	tolerance	peaceful

Collective noun	Abstract noun	Adjective	Adverb

   /4

2. Change the tense of each sentence below into the tense written in brackets. Write the new sentence on the line.

   Example: I take evening classes in Spanish. (PRESENT PROGRESSIVE)
   I am taking evening classes in Spanish.

   a) Kristina and Lucas are on the school council. (SIMPLE FUTURE)
   _____

   b) We work hard at the rehearsal. (SIMPLE PAST)
   _____

   c) Jodie bounces on her trampoline. (PRESENT PROGRESSIVE)
   _____

   d) You tidy the sports equipment. (PRESENT PERFECT)
   _____

   /4

Grammar and punctuation

Section 2 Test 2 continued

3. Each sentence below is missing one or more apostrophes. Correct the sentences.

   a) They're all heading to Steffi's house to revise later.

   b) Please don't shout at me – just tell me what's the matter.

   c) My cat trapped its tail but luckily it's not hurt.

   d) The girl's mother told her daughters that they were not allowed to go to Lewis' party.

   /4

4. Read each sentence below and decide whether it is written in the active voice or the passive voice. Write **active** or **passive** on the line.

   a) My cousin accidentally broke the expensive vase. _____

   b) Next September, a new swimming pool will be built near our school. _____

   c) Quite by chance, we discovered a secret hiding place in our grandma's attic. _____

   d) When he visited Norway, Tom was overwhelmed by the beauty of the landscape. _____

   /4

5. Underline the preposition and circle the pronoun in each sentence.

   a) Please lean your umbrella against that wall, if you wouldn't mind.

   b) Having entered the foyer, they wiped their feet on the doormat.

   c) The cat waited outside the mouse's shelter, dreaming of gobbling her up.

   d) Everyone enjoyed toasting marshmallows beside the fire.

   e) Did anybody bring any popcorn to eat during the film?

   f) Lying sprawled across the comfy sofa, he closed his eyes.

   /6

Score:	Time taken:	Target met?

English Rapid Tests 6

Section 2 Test 3

Spelling and vocabulary

Target time: **8 minutes**

1. In each sentence below, there is a word that contains a silent letter. Underline the silent letter.

   Example: The police officer <u>k</u>nocked loudly on the door.

   a) Gratefully, the dog gnawed the bone.

   b) The writer used a pseudonym to hide his identity.

   c) You need a strong sense of rhythm to be a tap dancer.

   d) The cake was gone in seconds – only a few crumbs were left on the plate.

   e) The teacher asked us whether we had understood.

   f) I wrapped my scarf around my neck.

   /6

2. Decide which of the words in bold are the correct homophones for each sentence. Underline the <u>two</u> words.

   Example: I could <u>**see**</u> / **sea** the **cue** / <u>**queue**</u> from the entrance.

   a) Hoping to discover her birthday **presence** / **presents**, Laila **pried** / **pride** into her mother's wardrobe.

   b) Kaden pretended to be allergic to egg **yokes** / **yolks**, because he thought they tasted **vile** / **vial**.

   c) Kelly was sent to a **naval** / **navel** base just outside Glasgow for what would be a very **intents** / **intense** training programme.

   d) The jacket was made from a **coarse** / **course**, rough material, and didn't fit her properly, so she planned to **altar** / **alter** it.

   /4

20

Schofield & Sims

English Rapid Tests 6 Answers

Notes for parents, tutors, teachers and other adult helpers

- **English Rapid Tests 6** is designed for 11- and 12-year-olds, but may also be suitable for some children of other ages.

- Remove this pull-out section before giving the book to the child.

- Before the child begins work on the first test, together read the instructions headed **What to do** on page 2. As you do so, point out to the child the suggested **Target time** for completing the test.

- Make sure the child has all the equipment in the list headed **What you need** on page 2.

- There are three sections in this book. Each section contains two comprehension tests, two grammar and punctuation tests, and two spelling and vocabulary tests.

- Explain to the child how he or she should go about timing the test. Alternatively, you may wish to time the test yourself. When the child has finished the test, together work out the **Time taken** and complete the box that appears at the end of the test.

- Mark the child's work using this pull-out section. Each test is out of 22 marks and each correct answer is worth one mark unless otherwise stated in the answers. Then complete the **Score** box at the end of the test.

- For all spelling questions, the answer must be spelt correctly for the full mark to be awarded. Where applicable, answers need to be written in full sentences and correct grammar used for marks to be awarded.

- This table shows you how to mark the **Target met?** box and the **Action** notes help you to plan the next step. However, these are suggestions only. Please use your own judgement as you decide how best to proceed.

Score	Time taken	Target met?	Action
1–11$\frac{1}{2}$	Any	Not yet	Give the child the previous book in the series. Provide help and support as needed.
12–17$\frac{1}{2}$	Any	Not yet	Encourage the child to keep practising using the tests in this book. The child may need to repeat some tests. If so, wait a few weeks or the child may simply remember the correct answers. Provide help and support as needed.
18–22	Over target – child took too long	Not yet	
18–22	On target – child took suggested time or less	Yes	Encourage the child to keep practising using further tests in this book.

- After finishing each test, the child should fill in the **Progress chart** on page 40.

- Whatever the test score, always encourage the child to have another go at the questions that he or she got wrong – without looking at the answers. If the child's answers are still incorrect, work through these questions together. Demonstrate the correct technique if necessary.

- If the child struggles with particular question types or areas, help him or her to develop the skills and strategies needed.

Answers

Section 1 Test 1 (pages 4–5)

1. A
2. B
3. B
4. A
5. If there is not much sunlight the solar panel will only be able to produce a small amount of power, which needs to be enough for the motor to run if you want the robot to work on a cloudy day.
   Award 1 mark for references to the power of the motor being reliant on how sunny it is, and 1 mark for references to the motor making the robot move.
6. melting the motor with the heat from the soldering gun and allowing the paper clip legs to touch the wires
   Award 1 mark for each of the answers above. (Maximum 2 marks.)
7. The robot will work without completing step five, but if you want your robot to look like a cockroach the eyes/antennae are probably needed.
   Award 1 mark for answers stating that this step is not necessary for the robot to work, and 1 mark for references to the fact it is necessary if they want it to look like a cockroach.
8. follow or try or solder or align or uncoil or bend or glue or let
   Imperative verbs are used in instructions because they tell us what actions we need to take.
   Award half a mark for each correct imperative verb. (Maximum 1 mark.) Award 1 mark for a correct explanation.
9. Subtitles allow the reader to locate the information they need easily. or Bullet points to list individual items of equipment prevent anything from being overlooked. or The method being outlined in numbered steps means that the reader can see what to do next.
   Award half a mark for each feature mentioned. (Maximum 1 mark.) Award a further half a mark for each relevant suggestion as to how the feature achieves its goal. (Maximum 1 mark.)
10. a) Position
    b) upturned
    c) frenzied
    d) gigantic
    e) scuttling
    f) confront
    g) mayhem
    h) springs

Section 1 Test 2 (pages 6–7)

1. a) am travelling
   b) went
   c) has spent
   d) had eaten
   This question is testing the child's understanding of tense and verb–subject agreement.
2. a) Theo works in the library; his brother, Daniel, works in the supermarket.
   b) Michaela's car is fast; Alma's car is even faster!
   c) The large sign had the words 'KEEP OUT!' painted on it in red.
   d) The buffet was delicious and included the following: three types of salad, two platters of sandwiches and an assortment of desserts.
   This question is testing the child's ability to use semicolons, commas, inverted commas, colons and apostrophes correctly. Award half a mark for each item of punctuation correctly inserted.
3. a) belief
   b) wonder or wonderment
   c) anxiety or anxiousness
   d) excitement or excitation or excitedness
   e) jealousy
   f) grief
   This question is testing the child's ability to identify and spell abstract nouns.

A2   Schofield & Sims

Answers

4. a) debris, shipwreck
    b) at, skilful
    c) law, institute
    d) Saturday, playing

    This question is testing the child's knowledge of correct word order. Both correct words must be underlined in order for the mark to be awarded.

5. a) D, hot, sunny
    b) no error
    c) C, her sister, Mel,
    d) B, an astronaut

    This question is testing the child's ability to proofread and correct punctuation errors. Award 1 mark for each question part. Award only half a mark if the error is spotted but not corrected accurately.

Section 1 Test 3 (pages 8–9)

1. a) superficial
    b) joyful
    c) tranquillity
    d) invigorating

    This question is testing the child's knowledge of antonyms.

2. a) dwelling
    b) sentimental
    c) essence
    d) prudent

    This question is testing the child's knowledge of synonyms.

3. a) etc.
    b) Rd
    c) oz
    d) Capt.

    This question is testing the child's ability to use common abbreviations.

4. a) E, adequate
    b) D, prejudice
    c) D, desolate
    d) no error

    This question is testing the child's ability to proofread and spell words. Award 1 mark for each question part. Award only half a mark if the error is spotted but not corrected accurately.

5. a) fleet
    b) swarm
    c) troupe/class/group
    d) range
    e) flight
    f) litter

    This question is testing the breadth of the child's vocabulary; specifically, collective nouns.

Section 1 Test 4 (pages 10–11)

1. C
2. D
3. D
4. B
5. Meshak had fallen asleep and didn't notice that the load being carried by one of the mules was slipping.

    Award 1 mark for references to Meshak falling asleep, and 1 mark for references to a mule losing its load.

6. Informal language: 'Oi' or 'dolt' or 'nincompoop' or 'fool of a boy'

    Informal sentence structures: 'Oi!' (short exclamation) or 'can't' (contraction) or 'fool of a boy' (incomplete sentence) or 'that one – there – fifth one back!' (use of dashes)

    Award 1 mark for each of the examples given above. The child does not have to provide an example of language and an example of a sentence structure in order for both marks to be awarded. (Maximum 2 marks.)

Answers

Section 1 Test 4 (pages 10–11) continued

7. Otis means that Meshak should be grateful that Otis is his father, as otherwise Otis would abandon him.

   Award 1 mark for answers that demonstrate an understanding that Otis is telling Meshak to be grateful for the familial ties between them, and 1 mark for references to the fact that Otis would otherwise abandon Meshak.

8. 'Smooth-tongued' means that Otis is clever with his words/he knows what to say to get his own way and he can persuade and manipulate people when speaking to them.

   Award 1 mark for answers that demonstrate an understanding that Otis is good with his words, and 1 mark for references to him using this to get his own way/influence people.

9. Otis flatters and entertains each customer to gain their trust, meaning they think they are getting a bargain and pay him whatever he asks for.

   Award 1 mark for references to Otis flattering or entertaining his customers, and 1 mark for references to customers trusting him/thinking they are getting a bargain.

10. a) dangled
    b) fumbled
    c) cuffed
    d) jeered
    e) slunk
    f) vulnerable
    g) stared
    h) incomprehension

Section 1 Test 5 (pages 12–13)

1. "Hurry up, Joshi!" called his mother. "You don't want to be late for school – not again!" Joshi rolled out of bed, bleary-eyed and with ruffled hair, and staggered to the bathroom to wash his face. He caught a glimpse of himself in the mirror and was shocked at how tired he looked – he had bags under his eyes the size of potato sacks! "Well, that's what comes of staying up half the night on the Xbox," he thought to himself.

   This question is testing the child's ability to use speech marks, commas, dashes and exclamation marks correctly. Award half a mark for each item of punctuation correctly inserted. Deduct half a mark for each item of punctuation incorrectly inserted. (Maximum 6 marks.) A colon after 'looked', and a full stop after 'sacks' are also acceptable.

2. a) those
   b) quickly
   c) have
   d) any

   This question is testing the child's ability to use Standard English correctly.

3. a) enviously
   b) hungrily
   c) joyfully or joyously
   d) mistakenly

   This question is testing the child's ability to identify and spell adverbs.

4. a) combust (Light the kindling first to get that fire burning quickly.)
   b) leader (They admired Susie greatly for her shrewd judgement.)
   c) a (He went to the shops to buy presents for his best friend.)
   d) knows ("What kind of American accent does he have?" he asked.)

   This question is testing the child's knowledge of correct word order.

5. a) D, of her sister's
   b) C, art classes;
   c) A, "That's enough!"
   d) no error

   This question is testing the child's ability to proofread and correct punctuation errors. Award 1 mark for each question part. Award only half a mark if the error is spotted but not corrected accurately.

A4   Schofield & Sims

Answers

Section 1 Test 6 (pages 14–15)

1. a) cutlet
   b) contour
   c) adaptable
   d) inmate
   e) downcast
   f) poppies

   This question is testing the child's ability to spot how two words can go together to make a new word.

2. a) glance glee glide glower glue
   b) brawl brawn break bream breeze
   c) thread threat thrice thrill through
   d) marina mariner martyr marvel marvellous

   This question is testing the child's knowledge of alphabetical order.

3. a) vaccine
   b) intervene
   c) routine
   d) canteen

   This question is testing the child's ability to identify spelling errors and correctly spell words with **–een**, **–ene** and **–ine** endings.

4. a) **wre**tched
   b) **pio**neer
   c) res**ign**
   d) contr**ibu**te

   This question is testing the child's knowledge of word meanings and spellings.

5. a) gilt
   b) bales
   c) flue
   d) rued

   This question is testing the child's ability to distinguish between common homophones.

Section 2 Test 1 (pages 16–17)

1. A
2. B
3. D
4. C
5. Sawing holes in the canoe would make it sink in water.

   Award 2 marks for references to the canoe sinking. This question is testing the child's inference skills.

6. literature or the people who are trying to destroy them or frightening and troublesome beasts which live nearby or which is the most terrifying part of a beast

   Award 1 mark for each of the answers above. (Maximum 2 marks.)

7. Because teeth are used for eating children, and often their parents, and gnawing their bones.

   Award 1 mark for references to teeth being used for eating children and their parents, and 1 mark for references to 'gnawing their bones'.

8. If you are seeing the belly of the beast, you have probably already seen all of the other scary parts of the beast. It means the beast has trapped you so there is probably no hope for you.

   Award 1 mark for answers stating that you have already seen the teeth, claws and hair, and 1 mark for answers stating that you are trapped or that there is probably no hope for you.

9. ominous and humorous

   Award 1 mark for each correct box ticked. Deduct 1 mark for every extra box ticked.

10. a) orphans
    b) cramped
    c) portable
    d) upholstery
    e) scenery
    f) fastened
    g) encounter
    h) research

Answers

Section 2 Test 2 (pages 18–19)

1.

Collective noun	Abstract noun	Adjective	Adverb
host	confidence	ambitious	solemnly
band	trust	peaceful	wildly
gaggle	despair	immense	seldom
murder	tolerance	considerate	promptly

This question is testing the child's ability to identify collective and abstract nouns, adjectives and adverbs. Award 1 mark for 4–7 correct words; 2 marks for 8–11 correct words; 3 marks for 12–15 correct words and 4 marks for 16 correct words. (Maximum 4 marks.) Note that 'seldom' can also be an adjective, but the answer given is the only way in which the table can be completed using each word only once.

2. a) Kristina and Lucas will be on the school council.
    b) We worked hard at the rehearsal.
    c) Jodie is bouncing on her trampoline.
    d) You have tidied the sports equipment.

    This question is testing the child's understanding of tenses and verb–subject agreement.

3. a) They're all heading to Steffi's house to revise later.
    b) Please don't shout at me – just tell me what's the matter.
    c) My cat trapped its tail but luckily it's not hurt.
    d) The girls' mother told her daughters that they were not allowed to go to Lewis' party.

    This question is testing the child's ability to use apostrophes for contractions and to indicate singular and plural possession. Award half a mark for each correctly inserted apostrophe. In part **c**, also award half a mark for <u>not</u> inserting an apostrophe into the first 'its', as this is the possessive form, and an apostrophe is only required for the contraction of 'it is'. In part **d**, also accept Lewis's.

4. a) active
    b) passive
    c) active
    d) passive

    This question is testing the child's ability to correctly identify sentences in both the active and the passive voice.

5. a) against (preposition), you (pronoun)
    b) on (preposition), they (pronoun)
    c) outside (preposition), her (pronoun)
    d) beside (preposition), everyone (pronoun)
    e) during (preposition), anybody (pronoun)
    f) across (preposition), he (pronoun)

    This question is testing the child's ability to identify pronouns and prepositions. Award half a mark for each correctly underlined preposition or circled pronoun. (Maximum 6 marks.)

Section 2 Test 3 (pages 20–21)

1. a) **g**nawed
    b) **p**seudonym
    c) r**h**ythm
    d) crum**b**s
    e) w**h**ether
    f) **w**rapped

    This question is testing the child's ability to identify words with silent letters.

2. a) presents, pried
    b) yolks, vile
    c) naval, intense
    d) coarse, alter

    This question is testing the child's ability to distinguish between common homophones. Award half a mark for each correctly underlined homophone. (Maximum 4 marks.)

3. a) irreverent
    b) admire
    c) comforting
    d) stable

    This question is testing the child's knowledge of antonyms.

A6   Schofield & Sims

Answers

4. a) amp, kilogram (all the others measure distance/length)
    b) viral, choir (all the others describe something said aloud)
    c) human, chicken (all the others have more than two legs)
    d) stove, coriander (all the others are colours)

    This question is testing the child's vocabulary and their ability to identify common features of words in order to find the link.

5. a) auditorium
    b) rebellion
    c) analyse
    d) population

    This question is testing the child's ability to spell tricky words correctly.

Section 2 Test 4 (pages 22–23)

1. C
2. C
3. A
4. D
5. The headline uses simpler/more exciting/more informal language than the article. This is to make it attention-grabbing/appealing to readers to encourage them to read the article.

   Award 1 mark for references to the headline using simpler/more exciting language, and 1 mark for answers showing an understanding that this is because its purpose is to grab the reader's attention so that they read the article.

6. Previous studies have identified the chemical 'reward' being released, but this is the first study that has manipulated this process in order to change the way that people think.

   Award 1 mark for references to this study being the first to manipulate the reward circuitry demonstrated in previous studies, and 1 mark for references to this changing the way people think.

7. Their willingness to spend money shows that it was their actions, not just their tastes, that were changed. The implications of this are far-reaching because it could be used by doctors or businesses to influence other spending habits in the future.

   Award 1 mark for references to the willingness to spend money being evidence of a change in someone's behaviour/actions, and 1 mark for references to the study having wider implications (e.g. influencing other spending habits).

8. These disorders are reliant on the same part of the brain that scientists manipulated in this study, so the same science could be used to change the way people with these disorders feel, think and act.

   Award 1 mark for references to these disorders being reliant on the same part of the brain that was manipulated, and 1 mark for references to scientists being able to use the results of this study to treat those disorders.

9. **Either:** I think it would be a good thing, because it could help prevent addictions/treat existing health problems and it could make people like lots of different, new things that might be beneficial to them.

   Or: I think it would be a bad thing, because personal tastes are part of our personalities and it is not fair/ethical to mess around with people's tastes.

   Award 2 marks for an opinion followed by two valid reasons supporting that opinion. Also accept 'I don't know' if a reason is given for each side.

10. a) che mical
    b) con su ming
    c) th eo ry
    d) r hy thms
    e) int er pret
    f) pre dic tions
    g) fac tors
    h) as so ciate

Answers

Section 2 Test 5 (pages 24–25)

1. a) impractical
    b) illegal
    c) incomplete
    d) irregular
    This question is testing the child's ability to add a prefix to turn an adjective into its antonym.

2. a) I think it was thunder that we heard.
    b) I haven't/have not got any sweets left.
    c) I don't/do not want any of those cakes.
    d) My cousin taught me how to ride a scooter.
    This question is testing the child's ability to use Standard English.

3. a) gardener (subject), flowerbed (object)
    b) children (subject), books (object)
    c) Aldo (subject), patients (object)
    d) I (subject), notes (object)
    This question is testing the child's ability to identify the subject and object of a sentence. Award half a mark for each correctly underlined subject or circled object. (Maximum 4 marks.) The half mark should still be awarded if the child circles the whole noun phrase (e.g. 'the flowerbed'; 'some new reading books'; 'many patients'; 'all my thank-you notes').

4. a) is hoping
    b) was learning
    c) was chatting
    d) will be walking
    e) was dreaming
    f) will be taking
    This question is testing the child's ability to select the appropriate verb form when writing in the past, present or future progressive tense.

5. a) "Please forgive me for losing your keyring!" Ross implored his sister.
    b) "Please will/would you drive me to school, Mum?" asked Hari.
    c) "There is a hurricane on the way," announced the weather reporter.
    d) "My tooth hurts!" Evie exclaimed. "Can I go to the dentist, Dad?"
    This question is testing the child's ability to punctuate direct speech correctly. The word order may vary from the above but all punctuation must be correct for the mark to be awarded.

Section 2 Test 6 (pages 26–27)

1. forehead, before, headline, behead
    This question is testing the child's ability to spot how two words can go together to make a new word. Award 1 mark for each word. The four words can be written in any order.

2. a) United States of America
    b) pound
    c) dictionary (also accept dictation)
    d) Reverend
    This question is testing the child's ability to recognise common abbreviations.

3. a) imprecise
    b) racket
    c) cooperative
    d) disparage
    This question is testing the child's knowledge of synonyms.

4. a) propeller or propelled or propelling
    b) rebellious or rebelled or rebelling
    c) signalling or signalled or signaller
    d) equality or equalling or equalled
    e) metallic or metalled
    f) shrivelled or shrivelling
    This question is testing the child's ability to add a suffix to a word and change the spelling as appropriate.

5. a) We made **silhouette** puppets at school today.
    b) We sailed around the world in a luxury **yacht**.
    c) I love watching television on the sofa in my **pyjamas**.

A8

Schofield & Sims

Answers

d) I like to collect magnets as **souvenirs** of the different places I have visited.

This question is testing the child's ability to spell tricky words correctly.

Section 3 Test 1 (pages 28–29)

1. D
2. A
3. C
4. D
5. They are the phantoms/ghosts/spirits inside the house. They listen to the Traveller's voice/noises from outside but do not say anything in return.

   Award 1 mark for references to the ghosts/spirits or phantoms, and 1 mark for references to them listening to the traveller but not speaking.

6. 'forest's ferny floor'

   The alliteration draws the reader's attention to that line or makes the words of the poem flow well or evokes the sound of the horse grazing or emphasises the sound of the horse chewing against the silence of the night.

   Award 1 mark for correctly identifying 'forest's ferny floor', and 1 mark for referring to one or more of the effects above. (Maximum 2 marks.)

7. It suggests there is a large group of listeners or that the phantom listeners were the original occupiers of the house when they were alive or that the listeners are hosting the Traveller as it is their house that he has come to.

   Award 2 marks for any one of the above explanations.

8. The Traveller realises that there aren't any people in the house, but he does not think that it is empty because he can feel the presence of the phantoms 'in his heart'/he says to 'Tell them I came'.

   Award 1 mark for answers that state that the traveller does not think the house is empty, and 1 mark for answers explaining that he can sense the phantoms or that he addresses them.

9. 'his horse in the silence champed the grasses' or 'Stood listening in the quiet of the moonlight To that voice from the world of men' or 'Their stillness answering his cry' or 'Though every word he spake Fell echoing through the shadowiness of the still house' or 'And how the silence surged softly backward, When the plunging hoofs were gone'

   In highlighting that only the Traveller is making any sound, the contrast creates a sense of eeriness by emphasising the mystery of the listeners who are not answering him.

   Award 1 mark for an appropriate example from the poem, and 1 mark for an explanation as to why this is effective.

10.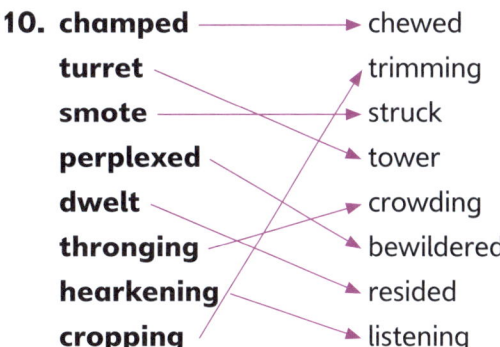

Section 3 Test 2 (pages 30–31)

1. **a)** Paulina asked her grandad if he would (be able to/please) bake her a cake for her party.

   b) Simon declared that he was going to enter the drawing competition.

   c) Jayden shrieked that there was a gigantic spider in the bath.

   d) The vet told the dog's owner that with plenty of rest, Amber/the dog would make a full recovery.

   This question is testing the child's ability to change a sentence from direct to indirect speech. Wording and word order may vary slightly from that given in the example answers above.

Answers

Section 3 Test 2 (pages 30–31) continued

2.
   a) yelped (She pursued the foxes into a deep glen.)
   b) stage (Becky delivered a powerful monologue, making the whole audience weep.)
   c) splash (His mother shouted, "Well done!" as he swam the length of the pool underwater.)
   d) game (After shuffling the pack, she dealt seven cards to every player.)

   This question is testing the child's knowledge of correct word order.

3.
   a) preposition, determiner
   b) noun, adjective
   c) verb, preposition
   d) adjective, adverb

   This question is testing the child's ability to identify different parts of speech. Award half a mark for each correct word class.

4.
   a) B, Vera's party
   b) C, three stations:
   c) E, her teacher
   d) C, and I have lots

   This question is testing the child's ability to proofread and correct punctuation errors. Award 1 mark for each question part. Award only half a mark if the error is spotted but not corrected accurately.

5.
   a) activate
   b) create
   c) lose
   d) replicate
   e) empathise
   f) anticipate

   This question is testing the child's ability to change adjectives and nouns into verbs. In part e, also accept 'empathize'.

Section 3 Test 3 (pages 32–33)

1.
   a) snippet
   b) carpet
   c) petting
   d) puppet

   This question is testing the child's ability to spot how two words can go together to make a new word.

2.
   a) no error
   b) E, pneumonia
   c) C, quotation
   d) D, hypocrite

   This question is testing the child's ability to proofread and spell words. Award 1 mark for each question part. Award only half a mark if the error is spotted but not corrected accurately.

3.
   a) inattentive
   b) irreconcilable
   c) misapprehend
   d) unfathomable

   This question is testing the child's knowledge of forming antonyms by adding appropriate prefixes.

4.
   a) observant
   b) frequent
   c) radiant
   d) innocent
   e) expectant
   f) obedient

   This question is testing the child's ability to spell words ending in **–ant** and **–ent**.

5.
   a) featherweight, insubstantial (all the others describe actions that create fire)
   b) button, shoelace (all the others mean 'to move quickly')
   c) funnel, cymbal (all the others are types of line/are related to direction)
   d) yen, dollar (all the others are synonyms for 'beat')

   This question is testing the child's vocabulary and their ability to identify common features of words in order to find the link.

Answers

Section 3 Test 4 (pages 34–35)

1. C
2. B
3. A
4. C
5. on the beach, in the road, on lawns, in homes, in swimming pools, in the sea

   Award 1 mark for each correct answer from the above. (Maximum 2 marks.)
6. 'like a human shish kebab'

   Award 2 marks for a correct answer.
7. The dome was 'impenetrable' and no one understood it, so they knew their relatives could be trapped inside for a long time.

   Award 1 mark for references to the dome being impenetrable/no one understanding the dome, and 1 mark for answers demonstrating an understanding that the Families' relatives could be trapped for a long time.
8. She had been called to the scene to explain the dome and realised it could take months or years.

   Award 1 mark for references to Dr. Heather Darby being a scientist who had been asked to explain the dome, and 1 mark for references to the work taking a long time.
9. impenetrable → impermeable
   jaunt → spree
   hastily → speedily
   sprawling → expansive
   resigned → stoic
   awe-inspiring → remarkable
10. Yes, she was happy because there was a nice beach and she found it exciting being surrounded by soldiers/police/scientists/media/the Families. She was also fascinated by the presence of the dome because it was mysterious.

    Award 1 mark for a positive answer and a further mark for each reason given. Reasons could include the beach; the excitement of the complex; the different people she was surrounded by; being near the Families; and the presence of the dome. (Maximum 4 marks.)

Section 3 Test 5 (pages 36–37)

1. a) which is a relatively new town
   b) where my grandparents live
   c) who runs our local newsagent
   d) that you borrowed from me (this morning)
   e) who is usually a very quiet child
   f) that had flecks of gold in it

   This question is testing the child's ability to identify relative clauses.

2.
Preposition	Pronoun	Verb	Noun
since	nobody	accelerate	tradition
alongside	someone	deliver	joke
aboard	those	accompany	sentence
despite	myself	unravel	rage

   This question is testing the child's ability to identify prepositions, pronouns, verbs and nouns. Award 1 mark for 4–7 correct words; 2 marks for 8–11 correct words; 3 marks for 12–15 correct words and 4 marks for 16 correct words. (Maximum 4 marks.) Note that 'joke', 'sentence' and 'rage' can also be verbs, and 'nobody' can also be a noun, but the answer given is the only way in which the table can be completed using each word only once.

3. a) graceful or gracious
   b) outrageous
   c) athletic
   d) decorative

   This question is testing the child's ability to change the spelling of a word in order to turn it into an adjective.

4. a) simple present
   b) present perfect
   c) future progressive
   d) past perfect

   This question is testing the child's ability to distinguish between the past perfect, present perfect, future progressive and simple present tenses.

Answers

Section 3 Test 5 (pages 36–37) continued

5. a) "Watch out**!**" shouted the man, as the ladder started to wobble dangerously.
    b) It was soon to be the main annual fundraising event at the donkey sanctuary**:** the charity ball**.**
    c) **T**he students thought it was time for a break**;** their teacher wanted them to finish the exercise first.
    d) "Your favourite school subjects are maths**,** science and art**,** aren't they?" Lucy asked Eva.

    This question is testing the child's understanding of the use of capital letters, semicolons, colons, full stops, exclamation marks, speech marks and commas. Award half a mark for each correctly inserted item of punctuation.

Section 3 Test 6 (pages 38–39)

1. a) generous
    b) fearless
    c) proud
    d) noble

    This question is testing the child's knowledge of synonyms.

2. a) lackadaisical, enthusiastic
    b) scathing, kind
    c) infamous, unknown
    d) orthodox, unconventional

    This question is testing the child's knowledge of antonyms.

3. a) soloist
    b) rainforest
    c) extremist
    d) furthest
    e) specialist
    f) modest

    This question is testing the child's ability to spell words ending in **–est** and **–ist**.

4. a) wailed, faint
    b) flair, vain
    c) baron, frieze
    d) sear, meat

    This question is testing the child's ability to distinguish between common homophones. Award half a mark for each correctly underlined homophone. (Maximum 4 marks.)

5. a) iced icicle icing island isosceles
    b) election electric electrify electrocute element
    c) reader realistic reality reaper rearrange
    d) design designate despicable destiny destitute

    This question is testing the child's knowledge of alphabetical order.

This book of answers is a pull-out section from **English Rapid Tests 6**.

Published by **Schofield & Sims Ltd**,
7 Mariner Court, Wakefield, West Yorkshire WF4 3FL, UK
Telephone 01484 607080
www.schofieldandsims.co.uk

This edition copyright © Schofield & Sims Ltd, 2018
First published in 2018
Second impression 2020

Author: Siân Goodspeed. Siân Goodspeed has asserted her moral rights under the Copyright, Designs and Patents Act, 1988, to be identified as the author of this work.

British Library Cataloguing in Publication Data. A catalogue record for this book is available from the British Library.

All rights reserved. No part of this publication may be reproduced, stored in a retrieval system, or transmitted in any form or by any means, electronic, mechanical, photocopying, recording or otherwise, without either the prior permission of the publisher or a licence permitting restricted copying in the United Kingdom issued by the Copyright Licensing Agency Ltd.

Design by **Ledgard Jepson Ltd**
Printed in the UK by **Page Bros (Norwich) Ltd**

ISBN 978 07217 1434 9

Spelling and vocabulary

Section **2** Test **3**
continued

3. Underline the word in each set of brackets that is an antonym of the word in bold.

   Example: **peak** (wide <u>trough</u> tall)

   a) **pious** (irreverent porous sacred)

   b) **abhor** (detest greet admire)

   c) **harrowing** (comforting distressing ploughing)

   d) **volatile** (stable hostile furtive)

   /4

4. Two of the words in each set do not go with the other four. Underline these <u>two</u> words.

   Example: temperate <u>icy</u> balmy mild pleasant <u>bitter</u>

   a) kilometre mile yard amp inch kilogram

   b) spoken viral verbal oral choir articulated

   c) centipede human octopus chicken spider tiger

   d) stove hazel coriander ivory turquoise navy

   /4

5. The following words are spelt incorrectly. Write the correct spelling on the line.

   a) orditorium _____

   b) rebeleon _____

   c) analise _____

   d) populashun _____

   /4

Score: Time taken: Target met?

Section 2 Test 4

Comprehension

Target time: **8 minutes**

Read the text and answer the questions below.

From **The Independent: Scientists zapped people's brains with magnetic pulses and it changed their taste in music**

Stimulating someone's brain with magnetic pulses is enough to change their taste in music, according to new research.

Using a non-invasive technique called transcranial magnetic stimulation, scientists managed to change the enjoyment of music felt by their subjects.

Not only did the treatment alter the way participants rated music, it even affected the amount of money they were willing to spend on it.

Showing that the way people value music can be changed using this technique is "an important – and remarkable – demonstration that the circuitry behind these complex responses is now becoming better understood," said Professor Robert Zatorre, a neurologist at Canada's McGill University and senior author of the *Nature Human Behaviour* study.

The circuitry in question is found in a part of the brain called the left dorsolateral prefrontal cortex.

Previous brain imaging studies have demonstrated that stimulation of this region leads to the release of a substance called dopamine, which acts as a chemical 'reward'. Other studies have shown that pleasurable music engages reward circuits in the brain.

But this is the first time anyone has manipulated this circuitry to change the way people think.

When the scientists used 'excitatory' stimulation on the target brain region, the participants reported that they liked the music they were listening to more, and when 'inhibitory' stimulation was used they liked it less.

These results played out in the participants' spending as well. The participants were willing to spend more on music following excitatory stimulation, and less following inhibitory stimulation.

All of the changes were only temporary.

Professor Zatorre thinks that this work could be applied to treat conditions as diverse as addiction, obesity and depression, because such disorders also rely on the brain's reward circuitry.

"Showing that this circuit can be manipulated so specifically in relation to music opens the door for many possible future applications in which the reward system may need to be up- or down-regulated," he said.

Write **A**, **B**, **C** or **D** on the answer line.

1. Who are the 'participants' mentioned in line 8?
   A the scientists who conducted the study
   B the mice who were being tested
   C the people whose brains were 'zapped'
   D the musicians who composed the music

   _____ /1

2. Which of these does the study <u>not</u> help scientists to understand?
   A how the brain's reward circuitry works
   B how to temporarily alter thoughts
   C how to permanently change music tastes
   D how to treat depression

   _____ /1

3. What was the 'target brain region' in the study?
   A the left dorsolateral prefrontal cortex
   B the neurologist
   C the transcranial magnetic stimulator
   D the brain imaging studies

   _____ /1

4. Which of the following acts as a chemical 'reward' in the brain?
   A magnetic pulses
   B pleasurable music
   C excitatory stimulation
   D dopamine

   _____ /1

Comprehension

Section 2 Test 4 continued

5. How does the language of the headline differ to the rest of the article? Why do you think this is?

_____

_____ /2

6. Why is this study of the brain's reward system different to those conducted in the past?

_____

_____ /2

7. Why do you think it is significant that participants were willing to spend more money on music after being 'zapped', rather than simply saying they liked it?

_____

_____ /2

8. In your own words, explain why Professor Zatorre believes the study will have important consequences for the treatment of addiction, obesity and depression.

_____

_____ /2

9. Do you think it would be a good thing or a bad thing if scientists were able to alter people's tastes permanently? Give <u>two</u> reasons.

_____

_____ /2

10. The following passage explains why people enjoy listening to music, but the words in bold have some letters missing. Fill in the letters of these incomplete words so that the passage makes sense.

Dopamine is a **a) c___ ___mical** released by our brain to make us feel pleasure when we do something that aids our survival, like **b) con___ ___ming** food. It is also released when we listen to music. One **c) th___ ___ry** as to why this happens is that, as we listen to music, we build expectations about the sounds and **d) r___ ___thms** that we will hear next. Animals must **e) int___ ___pret** signs of danger correctly in order to avoid predators, so our brain rewards us when we make accurate **f) pre___ ___ctions**. However, the way we feel when we listen to music is also influenced by **g) f___ ___tors** such as the memories we **h) as___ ___ciate** with a piece of music and who we are with when we hear it. /8

| Score: | Time taken: | Target met? |

Section 2 Test 5

Grammar and punctuation

Target time: 8 minutes

1. Add a prefix to the beginning of each adjective to change it into its antonym. Write the new word on the line.

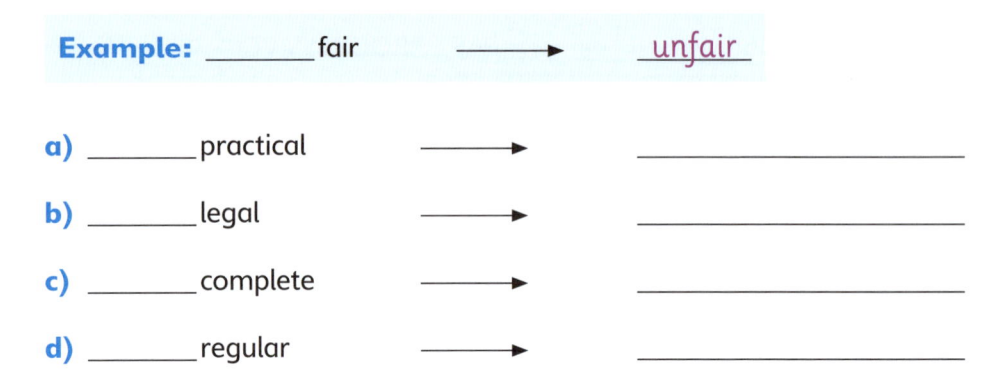

   Example: _____ fair ⟶ _unfair_

   a) _____ practical ⟶ _____

   b) _____ legal ⟶ _____

   c) _____ complete ⟶ _____

   d) _____ regular ⟶ _____

   /4

2. Write out each of the sentences below on the line using Standard English.

   a) I think it was thunder what we heard.

   _____

   b) I ain't got no sweets left.

   _____

   c) I don't want none of them cakes.

   _____

   d) My cousin learned me how to ride a scooter.

   _____

   /4

3. Underline the subject and circle the object in each sentence.

   a) The gardener was busy weeding the flowerbed.

   b) The children decided to choose some new reading books from the library.

   c) Aldo is a highly skilled surgeon who has operated on many patients.

   d) I was overjoyed to have finally finished writing all my thank-you notes.

   /4

24

Schofield & Sims

Grammar and punctuation Section **2** Test **5** continued

4. Change the missing verb to the tense given in brackets to complete each sentence. Write the missing verb form on the line.

Example: Li (help) _was helping_ her dad with the dinner. (PAST PROGRESSIVE)

a) Jo (hope) _____ to win the business award. (PRESENT PROGRESSIVE)

b) Alex (learn) _____ her lines for the school play. (PAST PROGRESSIVE)

c) I (chat) _____ to my friend when I was told off. (PAST PROGRESSIVE)

d) Next week, our class (walk) _____ ten miles to raise money for our school. (FUTURE PROGRESSIVE)

e) At first, I thought I (dream) _____ when I saw my favourite author in the street. (PAST PROGRESSIVE)

f) My uncle (take) _____ me to see the latest 'Star Battles' film when it is released. (FUTURE PROGRESSIVE)

/6

5. Change each of the following sentences into direct speech. Keep the tense the same. Write the new sentence on the line.

a) Ross implored his sister to forgive him for losing her keyring.

_____

b) Hari asked his mother if she would drive him to school.

_____

c) The weather reporter announced that there was a hurricane on the way.

_____

_____

d) Evie exclaimed that her tooth was hurting and asked her father if she could visit the dentist.

_____

_____

/4

| Score: | Time taken: | Target met? |

Section 2 Test 6

Spelling and vocabulary

Target time: 8 minutes

1. Mix and match the words in the box to make four new words. Write each new word on a line.

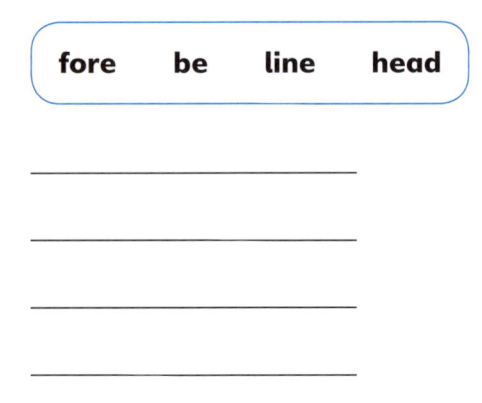

| fore   be   line   head |

_____

_____

_____

_____

/4

2. Write out each abbreviation below in full on the line.

Example: St.   _Saint_

a) USA   _____

b) lb   _____

c) dict.   _____

d) Rev.   _____

/4

3. Underline the word in each set of brackets that is a synonym of the word in bold.

Example: dull   (bright   chilly   <u>dismal</u>)

a) **vague**   (scientist   calm   imprecise)

b) **cacophony** (racket   false   quiet)

c) **amenable**   (cooperative   grand   discussion)

d) **criticise** (uplift   disparage   deity)

/4

26

Schofield & Sims

Spelling and vocabulary

Section **2** Test **6**
continued

4. Add a suffix from the box below to complete each word. You may need to change the spelling of the word. Write the new word on the line. There is more than one correct answer for each word.

> –ious   –ing   –ic   –ity   –ed   –er

a) propel_____ ⟶ _____

b) rebel_____ ⟶ _____

c) signal_____ ⟶ _____

d) equal_____ ⟶ _____

e) metal_____ ⟶ _____

f) shrivel_____ ⟶ _____

/6

5. In each sentence below there is an incorrectly spelt word. Find the word, underline it and then write out the sentence on the line with the word spelt correctly.

a) We made silhuoette puppets at school today.

_____

b) We sailed around the world in a luxury yauht.

_____

c) I love watching television on the sofa in my pijamas.

_____

d) I like to collect magnets as souveneers of the different places I have visited.

_____

_____

/4

Score: Time taken: Target met?

English Rapid Tests 6   27

Section 3 Test 1

Comprehension

Target time: **8 minutes**

Read the text and answer the questions below.

The Listeners, by Walter De La Mare

"Is there anybody there?" said the Traveller,
Knocking on the moonlit door;
And his horse in the silence champed the grasses
Of the forest's ferny floor:
5   And a bird flew up out of the turret,
Above the Traveller's head:
And he smote upon the door again a second time;
"Is there anybody there?" he said.
But no one descended to the Traveller;
10   No head from the leaf-fringed sill
Leaned over and looked into his grey eyes,
Where he stood perplexed and still.
But only a host of phantom listeners
That dwelt in the lone house then
15   Stood listening in the quiet of the moonlight
To that voice from the world of men:
Stood thronging the faint moonbeams on the dark stair,
That goes down to the empty hall,
Hearkening in an air stirred and shaken
20   By the lonely Traveller's call.
And he felt in his heart their strangeness,
Their stillness answering his cry,
While his horse moved, cropping the dark turf,
'Neath the starred and leafy sky;
25   For he suddenly smote on the door, even
Louder, and lifted his head: —
"Tell them I came, and no one answered,
That I kept my word," he said.
Never the least stir made the listeners,
30   Though every word he spake
Fell echoing through the shadowiness of the still house
From the one man left awake:
Ay, they heard his foot upon the stirrup,
And the sound of iron on stone,
35   And how the silence surged softly backward,
When the plunging hoofs were gone.

Write **A**, **B**, **C** or **D** on the answer line.

1. How many times in total does the Traveller knock on the door?
   A   twice
   B   four times
   C   once
   D   three times

   _____ /1

2. What rhyme scheme does the poem use?
   A   ABCB
   B   ABAB
   C   AABB
   D   The poem does not use a rhyme scheme.

   _____ /1

3. At what time of day is the poem set?
   A   dawn
   B   afternoon
   C   night-time
   D   twilight

   _____ /1

4. In line 34, what is making 'the sound of iron on stone'?
   A   the Traveller's foot in the stirrup
   B   the one man who is awake in the house
   C   the Traveller knocking on the door
   D   the horse's shoes striking the ground

   _____ /1

Comprehension Section 3 Test 1 continued

5. Who are 'the listeners', and why do you think the poet calls them this?

   _____
   _____ /2

6. Give an example of alliteration in the first four lines of the poem and describe its effect.

   _____
   _____ /2

7. In line 13, why do you think the poet describes the group of listeners using the word 'host'?

   _____
   _____ /2

8. By the end of the poem, does the Traveller think the house is empty? Explain your answer.

   _____
   _____ /2

9. The poet frequently contrasts the noise the Traveller and his horse are making with the silence of the listeners inside. Give an example from the poem and explain why it is effective.

   _____
   _____ /2

10. The words on the left in blue can all be found in the text. Draw lines to match each word with its meaning in the text.

champed	chewed
turret	trimming
smote	struck
perplexed	tower
dwelt	crowding
thronging	bewildered
hearkening	resided
cropping	listening

    /8

Score: ____   Time taken: ____   Target met? ____

English Rapid Tests 6

Section 3 Test 2

Grammar and punctuation

Target time: 8 minutes

1. Change each sentence below into indirect speech. Write the new sentence on the line.

   a) "Would you be able to bake me a cake for my party, please?" Paulina asked her grandad.
   _____

   b) "I think," declared Simon, "that I'm going to enter the drawing competition."
   _____

   c) "There's a gigantic spider in the bath!" shrieked Jayden.
   _____

   d) "With plenty of rest, Amber will make a full recovery," the vet told the dog's owner.
   _____

   /4

2. The words in the sentences below have been jumbled up and an extra word has been added in that is not needed. Unjumble the sentences in your head so they make sense, and write the extra word on the line.

   Example: which yours when hat is?   _when_

   a) pursued she foxes yelped into the deep a glen.   _____

   b) delivered a Becky stage making monologue whole the audience, weep powerful.   _____

   c) mother shouted the pool his, "Well done!" as splash he swam length of underwater the.   _____

   d) player every pack seven dealt cards to, the game shuffling after she.   _____

   /4

3. Read the sentences below. Identify the word classes of the words in bold in each sentence and write the word classes on the lines.

   a) The robin flew **over** the children playing in **the** garden.   _____ _____

   b) The **lawn** looked much **better** after being mown.   _____ _____

   c) Pratik **polished** his teeth **with** his new toothbrush.   _____ _____

   d) The cold, **crisp** autumn day was **almost** at an end.   _____ _____

   /4

Grammar and punctuation

Section 3 Test 2 continued

4. Some of the following sentences contain a punctuation error. If you spot an error, circle the letter above it and then write out that part of the sentence correctly on the line. If there is no error, write **no error** on the line.

a)

A	B	C	D	E
Maureen left	Veras party	early because	she was	rather tired.

_____

b)

A	B	C	D	E
The train	stopped at	three stations	Hull, Selby	and Leeds.

_____

c)

A	B	C	D	E
"What's the	last lesson	of the day?"	Sienna asked	her Teacher.

_____

d)

A	B	C	D	E
I love fancy	dress parties	and I have lot's	of different	costumes.

_____

/4

5. Turn each noun or adjective into a verb by adding, changing or removing a suffix. Write the verb on the line.

Example: winner ⟶ _win_

a) active ⟶ _____

b) creation ⟶ _____

c) loss ⟶ _____

d) replica ⟶ _____

e) empathy ⟶ _____

f) anticipation ⟶ _____

/6

Score: ____ Time taken: ____ Target met? ____

Section 3 Test 3

Spelling and vocabulary

Target time: 8 minutes

1. Find one word that can be added before or after all four words below to make four new words. Write each new word on the line.

   a) snip   _____

   b) car   _____

   c) ting   _____

   d) pup   _____

   /4

2. Some of the following sentences contain a spelling error. If you spot an error, circle the letter above it and then write the correct spelling on the line. If there is no error, write **no error** on the line.

   a)

A	B	C	D	E
The lecturer	gesticulated	wildly to	emphasise	his point.

   _____

   b)

A	B	C	D	E
Jo is relieved	that her nan	has recovered	from her bout	of pnuemonia.

   _____

   c)

A	B	C	D	E
I learnt	how to use	quotatshun	marks in	English today.

   _____

   d)

A	B	C	D	E
Safira accused	her neighbour	of being a	hippocrite	and a liar.

   _____

   /4

32

Schofield & Sims

Spelling and vocabulary

Section 3 Test 3
continued

3. Add a prefix to the beginning of each adjective to change it into its antonym. Write the new word on the line.

   Example: _____ fair ⟶ _unfair_

   a) _____ attentive ⟶ _____

   b) _____ reconcilable ⟶ _____

   c) _____ apprehend ⟶ _____

   d) _____ fathomable ⟶ _____

   /4

4. Add **–ant** or **–ent** to complete each word. Write the word on the line.

   a) observ_____ ⟶ _____

   b) frequ_____ ⟶ _____

   c) radi_____ ⟶ _____

   d) innoc_____ ⟶ _____

   e) expect_____ ⟶ _____

   f) obedi_____ ⟶ _____

   /6

5. Two of the words in each set do not go with the other four. Underline these <u>two</u> words.

   Example: temperate <u>icy</u> balmy mild pleasant <u>bitter</u>

   a) featherweight light ignite insubstantial kindle spark

   b) button zip hurtle sprint shoelace race

   c) parallel horizontal funnel vertical cymbal diagonal

   d) yen strike pound dollar pummel batter

   /4

Score: _____   Time taken: _____   Target met? _____

English Rapid Tests 6

Section 3 Test 4

Comprehension

Target time: **8 minutes**

Read the text and answer the questions below.

Extract from **Monster, by Michael Grant**

One day the dome had simply appeared, a perfect sphere twenty miles in diameter which extended down beneath the ground as far as it rose into the sky. That dome was centred on a nuclear power plant, but encompassed vast tracts of forest, hills, farmland, ocean, and almost all of the town of Perdido Beach, California, which lay at the extreme southern end.

5 The instant the dome appeared (impenetrable, opaque, and utterly impervious to drills, lasers and shaped explosive charges), every single person fifteen years of age and older had been ejected.

Ejected.

They had popped up on the beach, in the road, on lawns, in homes, in people's swimming pools. Some had been injured or killed, suddenly materializing in front of speeding trucks. Some had drowned, finding themselves without
10 warning a mile out to sea. A few had materialized in solid objects, with one man skewered by a lamppost, like a human shish kebab. And some had been turned inside out, for reasons that no one had understood then or later.

One of the first scientists to be called to the scene to explain this incredible, impossible, and yet terrifyingly real phenomenon was Dr. Heather Darby of Northwestern University, in Evanston, a suburb of Chicago. She had soon realized that this would be no overnight jaunt and that the study of the dome would take months if not years.

15 So Dr. Heather Darby had flown her daughter out to stay with her in the temporary housing complex hastily erected by the military.

For Shade Darby, thirteen years old, it had been wonderful. First and foremost, there was the beach. Evanston had a beach, but it did not compare to the long stretches of golden sand south of Perdido Beach. Then there was the excitement of being in a sprawling, makeshift compound teeming with soldiers and police and scientists and media
20 and, of course, the Families of the captives in the dome.

The Families. People capitalized it because everyone knew what that meant. They'd been all over TV, the Families. Hysterical at first, then angry, and finally depressed and resigned and hopeless.

But most of all for Shade there was the awe-inspiring, overwhelming presence of the dome itself. It was a mystery so profound that no human had yet come close to understanding it, not even her mother.

Write **A**, **B**, **C** or **D** on the answer line.

1. What was at the centre of the dome?
   - **A** a forest
   - **B** hills
   - **C** a nuclear plant
   - **D** the ocean

   _____ /1

2. Which town was almost covered by the dome?
   - **A** California
   - **B** Perdido Beach
   - **C** Chicago
   - **D** Evanston

   _____ /1

3. What happened to all the people over the age of fifteen?
   - **A** They were expelled.
   - **B** They were exterminated.
   - **C** They were eliminated.
   - **D** They were interjected.

   _____ /1

4. Which university was Dr. Heather Darby from?
   - **A** Perdido University
   - **B** Evanston University
   - **C** Northwestern University
   - **D** Chicago University

   _____ /1

Comprehension　　　　　　　　　　　　　　　　　　　　　　　Section **3** Test **4**
continued

5. Name <u>two</u> of the places where the people who had been ejected from the dome materialised.

_____

_____ /2

6. Look at lines 8–11. Find a simile and write it on the line.

_____ /2

7. Why did the Families end up feeling 'resigned and hopeless'?

_____

_____ /2

8. Why did Dr. Heather Darby move near the dome, and why did she move her daughter there?

_____

_____ /2

9. The words on the left in blue can all be found in the text. Draw lines to match each word with its meaning in the text.

impenetrable	spree
jaunt	speedily
hastily	impermeable
sprawling	remarkable
resigned	expansive
awe-inspiring	stoic

/6

10. Was Shade Darby happy about moving to the temporary housing complex? Explain your answer.

_____

_____

_____

_____ /4

Score: ☐　　Time taken: ☐　　Target met? ☐

English Rapid Tests 6

Section 3 Test 5

Grammar and punctuation

Target time: **8 minutes**

1. Underline the relative clause in each sentence.

> **Example:** Rachel enjoyed the blueberry muffins <u>that her sister had made</u>.

a) My aunt lives in Stevenage, which is a relatively new town.

b) My parents are saving up for a trip to Australia, where my grandparents live.

c) I like the man who runs our local newsagent – he is very helpful and always smiling.

d) Could you please return the pen that you borrowed from me this morning?

e) Annabelle, who is usually a very quiet child, shrieked with laughter throughout the film.

f) At the beach yesterday, Daniel's younger brother found an unusual stone that had flecks of gold in it.

/6

2. Sort each word in the word bank into the correct word class by writing it into the table below. You may use each word only once.

Word bank

since	despite	deliver	myself
accelerate	joke	rage	accompany
someone	alongside	those	aboard
tradition	unravel	nobody	sentence

Preposition	Pronoun	Verb	Noun

/4

36 Schofield & Sims

Grammar and punctuation　　　　　　　　　　　　　　　　　　　Section **3** Test **5**
continued

3. Turn each word into an adjective by adding or changing the suffix. Write the adjective on the line.

   Example: win　⟶　_winning_

   a) grace　⟶　_____

   b) outrage　⟶　_____

   c) athlete　⟶　_____

   d) decorate　⟶　_____

   /4

4. Identify which tense each of the following sentences is written in and write it on the line.
   Choose from: **past perfect**, **present perfect**, **future progressive** and **simple present**.

   Example: Leo has read three books so far this summer.　_present perfect_

   a) When making bread, it is essential to knead the dough.　_____

   b) Unfortunately, Caleb has upset his best friend.　_____

   c) George will be buying a ticket before boarding the train.　_____

   d) I had hoped to attend my daughter's school play.　_____

   /4

5. Each sentence below is missing <u>two</u> items of punctuation. Correct the sentences.

   a) "Watch out shouted the man, as the ladder started to wobble dangerously.

   b) It was soon to be the main annual fundraising event at the donkey sanctuary the charity ball

   c) the students thought it was time for a break their teacher wanted them to finish the exercise first.

   d) "Your favourite school subjects are maths science and art aren't they?" Lucy asked Eva.

   /4

Score: ☐　　Time taken: ☐　　Target met? ☐

English Rapid Tests 6　　　　　　　　　　　　　　　　　　　　　　　37

Section 3 Test 6

Spelling and vocabulary

Target time: 8 minutes

1. Underline the word in each set of brackets that is a synonym of the word in bold.

   Example: dull   (bright   chilly   <u>dismal</u>)

   a) **magnanimous**   (huge   generous   animated)

   b) **intrepid**   (fearless   shy   fast)

   c) **haughty**   (comical   inaccurate   proud)

   d) **gallant**   (storyteller   noble   bully)

   /4

2. Underline the two words (one word in each set of brackets) that are antonyms.

   Example: (<u>up</u>   along   parallel)   (above   between   <u>down</u>)

   a) (lamentable   harried   lackadaisical)   (melancholic   harassed   enthusiastic)

   b) (exemplar   scathing   educated)   (kind   mocking   scholarly)

   c) (tepid   impish   infamous)   (mild   mischievous   unknown)

   d) (lavish   exile   orthodox)   (unconventional   outcast   extravagant)

   /4

3. Add **–est** or **–ist** to complete each word. Write the word on the line.

   a) solo_____   ⟶   _____

   b) rainfor_____   ⟶   _____

   c) extrem_____   ⟶   _____

   d) furth_____   ⟶   _____

   e) special_____   ⟶   _____

   f) mod_____   ⟶   _____

   /6

Spelling and vocabulary

Section **3** Test **6**
continued

4. Decide which of the words in bold are the correct homophones for each sentence. Underline the two words.

   Example: I could **see** / **sea** the **cue** / **queue** from the entrance.

   a) Tia **wailed** / **whaled** that she was going to **feint** / **faint** from the pain.

   b) Gabriel had a **flair** / **flare** for modelling, although some of his friends thought he was rather **vain** / **vane**.

   c) The **baron** / **barren** gazed in wonder at the elaborate **frieze** / **freeze** that was painted on the wall of the great hall.

   d) The recipe said to **sear** / **seer** the **meat** / **meet** in the pan before stewing it to make a casserole.

   /4

5. Write out the words in each row on the line so that they are in alphabetical order.

   Example: play place ploy plea plant   _place plant play plea ploy_

   a) isosceles icing island icicle iced

   _____

   b) element electric election electrocute electrify

   _____

   c) reality reaper realistic reader rearrange

   _____

   d) destitute design despicable destiny designate

   _____

   /4

Score:	Time taken:	Target met?

Progress chart

Write the score (out of 22) for each test in the box provided on the right of the graph.
Then colour in the row next to the box to represent this score.

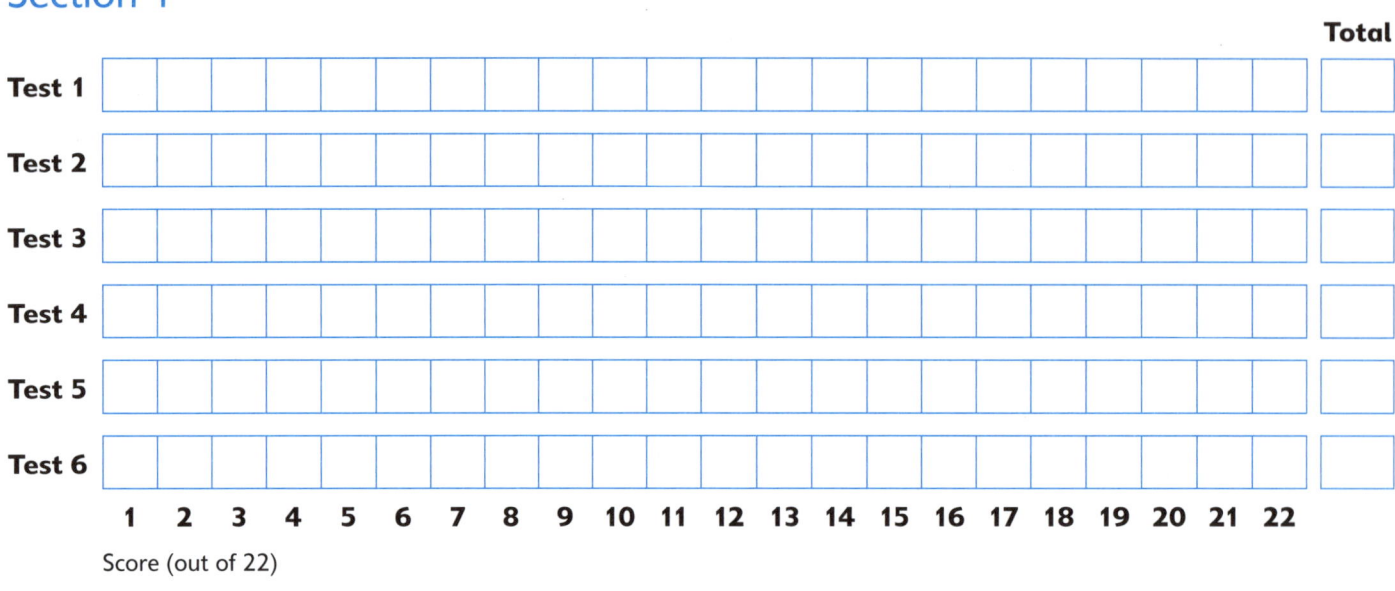

Section 1

		Total
Test 1		
Test 2		
Test 3		
Test 4		
Test 5		
Test 6		

1 2 3 4 5 6 7 8 9 10 11 12 13 14 15 16 17 18 19 20 21 22
Score (out of 22)

Section 2

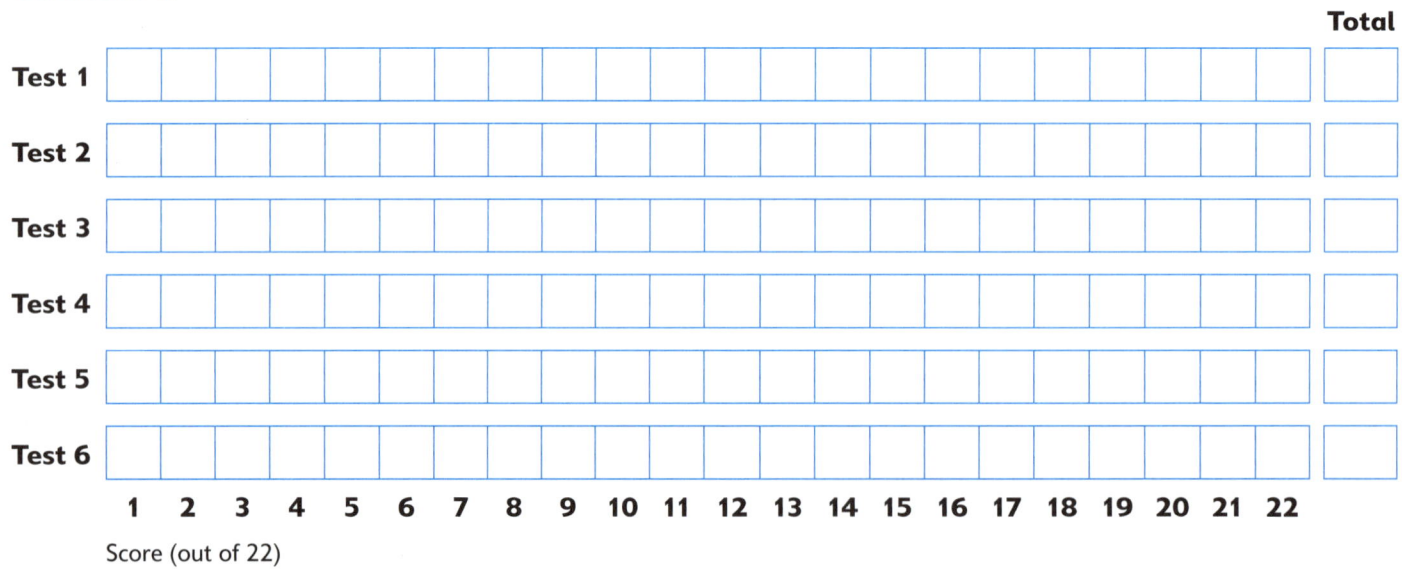

		Total
Test 1		
Test 2		
Test 3		
Test 4		
Test 5		
Test 6		

1 2 3 4 5 6 7 8 9 10 11 12 13 14 15 16 17 18 19 20 21 22
Score (out of 22)

Section 3

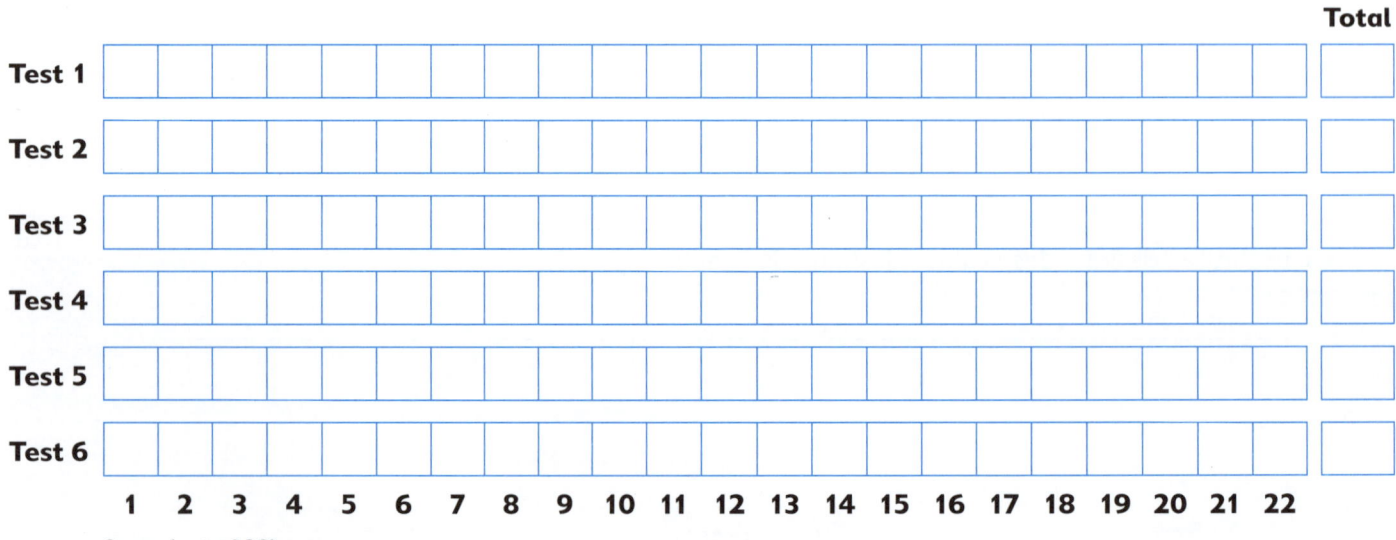

		Total
Test 1		
Test 2		
Test 3		
Test 4		
Test 5		
Test 6		

1 2 3 4 5 6 7 8 9 10 11 12 13 14 15 16 17 18 19 20 21 22
Score (out of 22)